Alpha and Omega

By the Same Author
(Published by Regency Press)
The Realms of Heaven
The Kingdom of Heaven

ALPHA AND OMEGA

by

THE ETERNAL SPIRIT

Regency Press (London & New York) Ltd.
Chaucer House, Chaucer Business Park,
Kemsing, Sevenoaks, Kent TN15 6PW

Copyright © 1997 by Margaret Clark
First Published 1997

This book is copyrighted under the Berne Convention. No portion may be reproduced by any process without the copyright holder's written permission except for the purposes of reviewing or criticism, as permitted under the Copyright Act of 1956.

ISBN 0 7212 0921 1

Printed and bound in Great Britain by
Buckland Press Ltd., Dover, Kent.

CONTENTS

		Page
Introduction		7
Chapter One	*"Is there anybody there?"*	9
Chapter Two	*The Cosmic Life Force*	15
Chapter Three	*The Many Levels of Evolution*	20
Chapter Four	*The Laws of Karma*	25
Chapter Five	*Self-Awareness*	32
Chapter Six	*Lost Worlds*	40
Chapter Seven	*The Search for Truth*	49
Chapter Eight	*When The Soul Flies Free*	57
Chapter Nine	*Past Life Memories*	63
Chapter Ten	*Alien Visitors*	68
Postscript		71

INTRODUCTION

When I pick up the pen, I feel a sense of unreality at times. But as the writing flows from another world, I realize how vast the universe is and how complex it all seems. Until it is explained, then it all falls into place as naturally as heaven and earth!

There is a great and loving presence all around me during the writings, and I am at times quite overcome at the wonder of it all.

It is not me who writes, but The Eternal Spirit, whose greatest desire is to pass on knowledge to all mankind, and I play a very small role indeed, by merely holding the pen for the power to flow.

There are believers and disbelievers. And it matters not one jot, for in time, everyone will learn the true facts of the Universe.

I am indebted to The Eternal Spirit for teaching me so much. I am indeed on a very exciting voyage of discovery that for me has only just begun.

Margaret Clark

CHAPTER ONE

"Is there anybody there?"

There are a great number of people who believe in life after death. But very few people believe that communication is possible, between the so-called living person and the deceased, who most certainly is not dead. Because nothing ever truly dies, only changes.

Let me explain how it works from my side of life in the spirit world, which is where I live, alongside many other spiritual beings, and there are others who are not quite so spiritual. Our world is an existence beyond time and space, as it is known on the earthplane, and far more beautiful than you can imagine.

When a message comes from the spirit world, to a loved one on the earthplane, it can give great comfort to a bereaved person. It can also change their life.

Anyone who is willing to sit in the silence for a few moments each day, and ponder quietly on spiritual matters, and perhaps send out loving thoughts, that are always received by the soul they are meant for in the spirit world, will receive a response. This never fails.

When a spirit person picks up the vibration of loving thoughts being sent to them, and decides to draw close to that person, it is just a matter of leaving the place they are in to visit them.

Let us assume, that a young woman has recently lost her Mother through death of the body, and in her quiet moments sends out loving thoughts to her Mother, that she misses her very much.

The love is still there between them, nothing ever dies. Love always exists and can't be parted by death. Sometimes it is enhanced by the death of someone, when the soul left behind didn't realise just how much they truly loved them.

The daughter sits quietly in a chair, and thinks about how much she misses and loves her Mother who is not dead, but very much alive and happy in the spirit world. The Mother picks up her thoughts and returns to her and very often the presence of a spirit person is sensed.

The daughter suddenly becomes aware that her Mother is standing in front of her. But she can't hear what her Mother is saying. She can't see her Mother with the physical eyes. But she can sense her presence and knows that she is there.

The daughter can send out her loving thoughts to her Mother, and her Mother who can quite clearly see her daughter sitting in the chair, also sends out waves of love, and thoughts go directly to the daughter who she still loves so dearly.

There are still so many people in a state of ignorance about the laws of spiritual matters. They often choose to ignore the truth thinking it doesn't concern them. How wrong they are, because it concerns every living soul. It is simply a state of awareness of what does exist in the universe.

I shall begin to explain about certain psychic matters first. Then we shall go on to the spiritual things that go hand in hand in the universe.

There are very few people who would admit to being psychic, and even less would admit to knowing anything about the spiritual realms that co-exist with the earthplane.

It is a medium's job to share and explain that which she receives from her guide, and other spirit persons, etc., but also that which she knows to be psychic, and nothing at all to do with the spirit world, although it is all linked by different energy fields.

And there are some people who would rather ignore the unseen, but definitely sensed by them, and pretend it doesn't exist. Death comes to everyone, so one might as well face it, knowing that it is but the passing from one phase, into another in the spirit world.

There are many levels of understanding, and many confused ideas about the psychic and spiritual matters. It is not always easy to believe if no proof is ever given. But someone with a closed mind will never learn one single thing about spiritual things, preferring to remain feeling safe and sound in their world of matter.

It is frequently found that an awakening, or a psychic happening occurs when someone dies, or if there has been a tragedy, murder, etc.

Then strange things can begin to happen. Sadness is like a great wet blanket thrown over one's shoulders. It offers no comfort to anyone. There must be a time to grieve and for mental goodbyes to be said to the loved ones, who have entered the spirit realms.

It is for the poor souls who have died in a state of ignorance and fear, and sometimes even terror, because they cannot comprehend what has happened to them. At this stage they are truly lost and totally unaware that they are free of all their earthly shackles and their suffering is indeed over.

This is when the power of healing comes in. They are taken to a place of rest, filled with harmonious energies and the most beautiful colour vibrations that gently flow all around.

The healing process can sometimes be a very slow business, on the other hand it can also be very quick. But when someone realizes that they are not dead, but very much alive. Then the questions begin!

It is so much easier for these poor souls if they knew that life was eternal in the first place, instead of arriving in a state of mental confusion, not realizing that they are alive and well and free from the illness that ended their physical life.

However, sometimes a person's state of mind can think they still have the illness that they died with, and can still show symptoms of the disease. But not for long, for they very soon become aware that they can't die, as loved ones greet them, and spiritual beings and friends, who they knew during their physical life, also welcome them, proving they have not died either.

It is often a very joyous occasion when realization dawns, and their first thought is to tell their loved ones left behind, and often still grieving. But they very rarely can see or hear their loved ones, trying so desperately to get their very important message across that they are not dead.

They do not like it when this happens, to be ignored by someone who one has loved during their lifetime on earth. Then to suddenly realize that one can neither be seen nor heard, causes great heartache, and the loved one has no choice but to withdraw, until their loved one dies and they can be re-united in the spirit world. Then a great and wonderful meeting takes place.

There are times when a spirit will draw close to their loved one still living an earthly life, and because of their grief and feeling of loneliness the spirit lingers beside their partner, loved one, etc. and refuses to leave.

This can cause problems. Sometimes the soul who has left his physical body behind, is afraid to go anywhere or explore the new spiritual realms he has suddenly found himself in.

Then God's work begins. A request goes out to great spiritual beings, asking for their help with the lost soul, who is clinging desperately to his loved one and is unable to leave for a variety of reasons.

A medium is also asked to help in this unhappy situation. The lost soul is urged to go forward into the light, that is there for everyone if they look. Living and dying is as natural as nature, and has been going on since time began, and is all part of progression of the soul. Who would want an earthly life to last for ever?

The many myths and legends that still exist, concerning what happens to someone's soul when the body dies, is still so unrealistic. It is almost laughable, were it not for the grief and suffering associated with the death of a loved one, which in many cases is a blessed relief. It is how a person lives his or her life, that decides exactly what plane of understanding they will go to. It may be a very spiritual level indeed, or it may not!

There are some very evil people upon the earthplane, who still perpetrate their wicked actions upon other poor innocent souls. These people who still exist in their physical life, will be absolutely horrified, if they could see what lies ahead for them when they too die, as everyone will sooner or later.

There are many levels of understanding in the spiritual realms, and ignorance is not one of them. The truth is always given to whoever asks for it, unless a lost soul decides to interfere, he is then dealt with and sent packing in no uncertain terms. The truth is always given no matter what the circumstances.

There are some mediums and psychics living on the earthplane, who choose to give spirit messages, but also to add their own little bit, which is often a misinterpretation of the truth. This is often well meant but quite wrong. If the spirit visitor wanted to say it the way the medium tells it, with her own little bits in, then he or she, would have said so in the first place. It is all due to lack of understanding.

There are more and more people becoming aware now than ever before, unless we go back far enough to Atlantis, when the the souls there knew of great things and explored all avenues of truth. Almost everyone in Atlantis was mediumistic, if not mediumistic, then extremely psychic. Everyone had the spiritual knowledge of paranormal things, as it is so often called now in present time on the earthplane. But in Atlantis it was almost common knowledge to know about the spiritual planes of understanding. It was very valuable information given to them, and vital to know of these very important matters, because it represented the truth, but they were also very advanced souls indeed.

The city of Atlantis was buried beneath the sea. It was an end to a community of people who had existed a very long time ago.

However, their knowledge has carried on into eternity, and it has passed down through the centuries to help people today.

There was a time when there were no Gods or idols, but only the spiritual laws, that represented the truth that goes far beyond the mere confines of religion.

Then the time came when craven images and idols began to be falsely worshipped, knowledge took a downward tilt, and ignorance and fear began to creep in. This began when christianity raised its ugly head, and the truth began to be distorted out of all reason. There were even sacrifices made in the name of a *God*! Preposterous! Everything began to be ruled in a very different way. The spiritual laws began to be forgotten and other religions began to take over.

There is money and power in religion, quite apart from all the deception that is still going on in the name of God.

However, there are still simple loving souls who believe and know beyond all shadow of doubt that money is not always the deciding factor, as so many people seem to think. Great things have been achieved without money ever exchanging hands.

The power of prayer has much more effect in the spiritual realms than money ever has. Those who put a price on their so-called spiritual work, will have to learn that it will have to be paid back, pound by pound, until nothing that has been taken is still owed.

There are laws in the Universe that cannot be altered to suit anyone. It is for the benefit of all mankind that these laws exist.

CHAPTER TWO

The Cosmic Life Force

My world is a vast and wondrous place, where there is much to learn. My life is a voyage of exciting discoveries, where all is revealed in my search for the truth. And I share my new found knowledge with all I meet, at their request.

I divulge every single scrap of information, and others do the same with me. We pool our knowledge, secrecy does not exist in my world, like it does on the earthplane. There are no chosen few. We are all equal in the eyes of God.

There are many curious people on the earthplane who gaze heavenwards, and wonder if life really does exist out there amongst the stars. If so, why can't they see them? Why can't they communicate with them? And if alien life forms exist, are they harmful or benevolent? The questions pour into the Universe. How they long for some sign, or to spot an alien space craft.

There are certain people on the earthplane, who have a very limited knowledge of extraterrestrials, and refuse to share it with others, who long to know more about what exists in outer space.

After all, they have as much right as anyone else on the earthplane to know what exists in their Universe.

These people in power, wrongly assume that other people would panic, if told an alien space ship had landed on the earthplane.

In the Arizona desert in the past, a flying saucer shaped spacecraft made a crash landing there. All its passengers were killed outright, no one survived. But was the knowledge shared? No it was not! Instead it was shrouded in a great mystery, and certain scientists were asked to investigate the space ship. Nothing of any great interest was found, because upon contact with the earth's atmosphere disintegration took place.

However, the space ship itself was taken to a secret place for further investigation, and it is still there. But no information for public interest was ever given.

These people who are in a position of power who decided what should be revealed and what should be kept secret, are betraying their position of trust, to the very people who elected them in the first place.

It is their misguided judgement that makes them act this way. Just think if everyone on the earthplane had access to all the information that concerns them, wouldn't that be a far better way of doing things?

To act openly and above board without secrecy, which leads to lies which in turn adds confusion and suspicion, everyone has a right to know what is going on, on their own planet. No one should take it upon themself to withhold information, knowledge belongs to everyone and should be shared. As it is in my world. What right has anyone to decide exactly what information should be passed on to people living on the earthplane, and exactly what should be kept secret?

It is a sin against God and the spiritual laws of karma to withhold information from anyone else. And a very high price will have to be paid when these people who are in a position of so-called power, eventually pass over into the spirit world as just another soul who has survived death!

They will soon find that they have no power over anyone else, as they had on the earthplane.

They will have to answer for their own actions, without being able to hide anything from anyone. All is known in the spirit world which is where I live.

Let me introduce myself. I am The Eternal Spirit who has dwelt in the heavenly Realms for a very, very long time indeed. I have progressed to quite a high state of consciousness and have learnt many exciting, and not so exciting things about the earthplane, including other planets that I visit from time to time. I am indeed a time traveller!

I travel beyond space and time. I can communicate on many levels with many other souls, who are most assuredly not in the spirit world, but live in different dimensions, such as Margaret Clark who lives in a physical body on the earthplane.

We work together in many ways, but the automatic writing, as she calls it, is the most dramatic to Margaret! Although she hears my thoughts quite plainly, and also the thoughts of other spiritual beings, who have chosen to work with Margaret on a spiritual level.

She asks many questions, and always the truthful answer is given, nothing is withheld. But if she does not ask, then no answer is given from our world, because we have gone beyond the desire to interfere with Margaret's free will, and anybody else's for that matter.

The lessons on the earthplane are endless, and the most important one of all is to learn that love is the greatest thing in the Universe. It transcends all mortal and physical ties. A life without love is indeed an aimless life, because nothing is achieved. Forgiveness is another of God's laws that begets love.

To ignore the things that exist in the Universe is to deny one's very existence, and it is the mind that is the key to the knowledge that is stored in the soul. And what raptures can be found, when realization dawns, that life is eternal.

There are so many exciting things in the Universe that exist to be explored by mankind, and very often it is only fear that holds someone back. Fear is ignorance, and can be dispensed with as soon as knowledge is given. Knowledge is the key to awareness.

There are many spiritualist churches run by mediums, who hold special services where communication from a soul in the spirit world can be given. When this happens to someone on the earthplane, their curiosity is aroused and this leads them to seek further for knowledge.

In these spiritualist churches, open circles are a place where information is very frequently given, from either the psychic world or spiritual Realms to someone sitting within the open circle.

These are very good teaching grounds for communication, but on a regular basis the mistakes and levels of communication can be very misleading at times, causing much laughter and often confusion. It is then up to the medium in charge to sort the matter out.

There is still a very great deal of difference between the psychic world and the spiritual Realms that exist. The psychic is something that every living soul upon the earthplane is capable of using.

It is a natural instinct. If it is not used, then mistakes will occur, and a soul may find themselves in deep trouble, simply because they did not listen to their own inner voice which is never silent! It is all a matter of being in tune with oneself.

These psychic abilities can be used to guide a soul to see clearly auras around other souls living upon the earthplane. All matter on the earthplane has an energy field called an aura.

This is quite easy to see if one persists psychically. It teaches one about the meaning of evolution, by learning about the wonderful and varied colours that exist everywhere upon the earthplane. Although not many see the wondrous spiritual colours that abound everywhere. Fancy living in a world of beautiful colours and not being able to see any of them. It is a blindness of the soul.

The only colours left are the earthly colours, still beautiful, but not half as wondrous as the energy fields that surround every living thing and all matter on the earthplane. Everyone should see some of these most wonderful colours at least once in their lifetime. It awakens one to the possibility that there is more in the Universe than one first supposed, and then the questions begin, quickly followed by knowledge which is what it is all about.

There are far too many religious superstitions on the earthplane, that often create needless heartache and suffering to so many people, and all in the name of God! There are still people who worship statues and think that it is a God, and others think they can confess their sins in church to someone living an earthly life, and they are automatically forgiven! What utter rubbish all this is. Yet, if one was to mention that they had either seen or heard a loved one who had passed over into the spirit world, well, what a reaction that can create!

It is still so unbelievable, that the natural process of communication with a soul in the heavenly Realms can be seen as evil. What utter rot!

All the attitude does is create fear, closes the mind to knowledge, and in fact, is seen as a crime against the holy laws of cause and effect which is to learn, learn, learn and grow into spiritual beings, without the fear of a pompous religious zealot breathing down one's neck.

These are lost souls indeed. They can only pray and expect God to help them rule others, and of course there is always a price to pay, money seems to walk hand in hand with religion. Many a poor hungry soul has walked into a church for comfort and found none, but a collection has been made, and that is all that is often achieved.

It can be very beneficial to have churches and other holy places, where people can go and pray to their God within the silence of their soul, which is how communication is made in the heavenly Realms, where I live very happily indeed, if I may say so.

It is a very sad state of affairs indeed, when someone who is in desperate need of help, turns to the clergy and receives nothing in the way of spiritual guidance. There have been occasions when a soul has knocked on God's door and not been allowed to enter, because of religious reasons.

There are far too many narrow-minded people in the religious order that condemn any form of communication with loved ones in the spirit world as evil. Just who are they kidding? And more to the point, what are they afraid of? It is about time all this hogwash was done away with and the truth revealed as it truly is.

CHAPTER THREE

The Many Levels of Evolution

I shall describe a little of my life in my spiritual Realm, which is beautiful beyond compare. There is nothing more glorious than the plane of understanding that I exist upon.

I work extremely hard for the benefit of all mankind. I try most earnestly to help all those poor lost souls who have no sense of direction in their lives, in both your world the earthplane, and mine the spiritual Realms.

The colours are beautiful and wondrous to behold, and difficult to describe. There are blues and greens, blending and merging with other wonderful colours, mauve, deep violet, autumn gold and sunshine yellow. Each colour resembles the purity of thought that is reflected in innocence and love in my world.

These feelings make my world a joyous place to be in. But it was not always so. There was a time long, long ago when I lived an earthly life, long before the laws of man were made and continents conquered. It was a time before the speech of man was ever made, long before life as a human being began. Although we had communication of another kind. You see I was then just a very small plant, evolution over the centuries has allowed me to grow and learn and become what I am now.

A highly evolved spiritual being, that lives in a very high and beautiful place of evolution. There is much to learn and I am still growing in knowledge and wisdom.

My world is not always where I stay. I travel quite extensively from one place to another. However, I always return home to my plane of existence. For instance, I visit the lower Realms where understanding is of a lower level and the colours and feelings on these lower levels are sometimes very nasty to feel and sense. These poor souls have never understood about their spiritual growth. They have lived selfish greedy lives during their time upon the earthplane.

They have committed a great many crimes against humanity during their many earthly lives, and so have returned to the plane of existence that they have earned by those deeds and acts of betrayal of their fellow man.

These souls will learn in time, but it can be a very slow business that can take centuries and centuries to learn that the sole purpose for an earthly life, is to become a spiritual soul of great kindness towards others.

Not until this lesson is learned will they progress. As they become kinder in their thoughts and deeds, so in turn their plane of existence will also become a brighter and happier place, because the laws of the Universe are all controlled, so that each soul earns exactly what they are given.

If they steal then the light all around them will become very dim indeed, but if they devote themselves to helping others in a caring and compassionate manner, and would never under any circumstances harm another living soul by the slightest thought or deed, and are pure in thought and action, these souls will ascend to a most beautiful place in the heavenly Realms.

They will have their own little home if that is what they desire, or they can merely live in a beautiful world without habitation, because we do not need sleep, neither are we ever ill because we are spirit only and not of the physical as it is on the earthplane.

The world I exist in most serenely, where troubled thoughts may never enter, is indeed Paradise.

There was also a time when I lived an earthly life and suffered much. I was just a poor soul who worked hard, ate little, because that is all there was.

I was a slave during the Roman Emperor Julius Caesar's reign and those were very cruel times indeed. I endured and died a very unhappy soul, until the time came when I found myself in a beautiful place unlike where I am now. But to me then it was like Paradise.

I remember quite clearly thinking I was dead, and yet as I looked all about me, I perceived the glorious terrain all around and simply could not understand it. Why was I here? Where was I? The questions went round and round in my head. Until a most spiritual being appeared before me and answered all my questions, and my confusion and fear left me.

I understood completely that I had merely passed from one existence into another much more peaceful one.

There was no sound of the whip that I had heard constantly throughout my life as a slave, and felt frequently upon my back for no apparent reason, except perhaps boredom and a cruel desire on the part of the soul in charge of slaves.

It was a life of Hell and I endured it and learned much. Many were the atrocities that I saw, and I prayed to God so often with tears in my eyes for the poor soul being tortured. They were barbaric times indeed. But that was only one lifetime.

I also had a life in Jerusalem during the time of Jesus. In fact, I knew him well, because I was also one of his disciples!

It was a time of learning and experiencing great and wondrous changes. The people had long awaited the coming of the Messiah, as they called him. When Jesus was born there was great rejoicing on the earthplane. But in the spiritual Realms great sadness, because of the suffering that Jesus had *chosen* to go through to help all mankind to love one another.

I walked with Jesus and talked with Jesus many, many times, and it was always a source of wonder to me that so beloved a soul should choose such an horrendous death upon the cross of man's ignorance.

I cried and helped to lift Jesus's body down from the cross. We wept as never before at the suffering of our beloved teacher. Yet, we knew that he could not die, but had merely departed from the earthplane into Paradise.

I felt very alone after that. It was the time that I helped to teach and tell other souls of the meaning of Christ, and to love one another, was the message that we should all live by.

I died at quite an old age. I was indeed in my eighties when I too passed on into Paradise. It was a great relief to me to return to my home in the heavenly Realms.

There were many beautiful souls waiting to greet me, Jesus also welcomed me and once again I cried with joy to be back where I belonged.

I have lived thousands of lifetimes upon the earthplane, and learnt and suffered much at the hands of man in the physical body. Some lives were more pleasant, but all involved suffering to some extent. What better way is there to learn about pain and suffering than to experience it oneself?

There have been lives on other planets that I have experienced, where beings unlike earth beings have lived. It was a time of great learning. And there have been so many lessons along the way of my different lives experience. But one of the most enlightening was my lifetime on another planet with beings who were so kind and intelligent. They just poured out love at whatever place they were in. It was quite an experience to be with them.

Their lifestyle was totally different to anything upon the earthplane.

It was a precious time of learning of the Universe, which they travelled around, rather like one jumps on a bus upon the earthplane. But their journeys were vast and exciting.

They could travel many millions of miles faster than anyone on the earthplane has achieved so far. They would travel up and down and around the various planets, or galaxies, as they used to call them.

I experienced many wondrous things as they were not just idle journeys of pleasure. They were exploration trips, journeys of knowledge and anyone who wished to go on any journey was quite welcome.

All were invited to share and pool their knowledge, nothing was kept hidden from anyone. Knowledge belonged to everyone and that is the true law of the Universe.

There are many worlds, many states of existence, just as there are many levels of understanding in my world, the spiritual Realms.

There are also evil doers and planets of darkness, that do not exist in a physical world, such as the earthplane.

These souls that can also travel the Universe are not of the light, but work in a twilight world of non-matter. These beings are rarely seen, but can occasionally be sensed, but this is extremely rare. They harm no one because they are of their own dimension, therefore cannot hurt or harm any other living soul, least of all on the earthplane.

These dark little creatures scurry about their domain, doing what harm and evil they can. All they do is hurt and harm each other. It is indeed a sad little world, but in time they will also learn and grow to be spiritual beings. But it will take aeons of time before even a spark of the divine light enters their dark souls.

Anyone who has the misfortune to meet them will feel the pain of their nasty dark little thoughts. But a soul who is of the light, will not be touched by them or harmed in any way. It is only those of similar thoughts who are affected by the disease of evil.

There are also many other light forms that exist in the Universe which is indeed vast. Why people on the earthplane often assume that they are the only lifeforms in the Universe, often amazes me at their naivety.

One day perhaps space travel will become a recognised thing, and space travellers will meet and share experiences in a very happy atmosphere. However, that is perhaps a long way off, for there are many souls who are quite aware of the people living upon planet earth, yet have no wish to meet or speak to them, because of their still unkindness and lack of understanding of each other.

The people who live on the earthplane, have still so much to learn about love and eternal life, which they seem to be so afraid of, even after all this time!

CHAPTER FOUR

The Laws of Karma

There are a great many souls who still live on the earthplane in a state of ignorance of the laws of the Universe.

These poor souls who shy away from learning about life after death, are denying themselves lessons that would help them to a greater understanding. It would also help them to come to terms with their own passing over into the spiritual Realms, or wherever they have chosen to go by their deeds and actions during their earthly life.

These people who constantly ignore God's laws are hiding the truth, not only from themselves, but also others. But if someone suddenly decides that they want to learn more about spiritual and psychic matters, their thoughts go out and are received by either their guide, or someone who wishes to help the soul by answering their unspoken, but quite clear *thought* request for knowledge.

A guide is a very wise soul indeed, who has chosen to guide and help someone upon the earthplane with spiritual lessons that they are curious about. The lessons about the spiritual laws are of great importance to all who seek for knowledge, because it helps to create a better understanding of why one is living a physical life upon the earthplane.

However, for those who only desire material things with no thought of spiritual things, will find that they are truly lost little souls indeed. As the saying goes, 'You can't take it with you.'

Material gain at the expense of spiritual knowledge is *useless*. But to seek for oneself a better class of living standards is a good thing.

The balance between rich and poor on the earthplane needs to be rectified.

If one is to steal from another soul, they in turn will suffer because they are merely stealing from themselves. To steal from someone else creates an effect of disharmony. Also it can create great waves of anger and frustration for the person who has been robbed, and perhaps this person has always led a blameless life, an honest life, and would never dream of stealing from anyone at all, no matter how impoverished they may have become. Honesty is integrity.

Those who steal from another soul living an earthly life are upsetting the balance upon the earthplane. It has often been said that good and evil are having a battle, and in a sense they are right. However, the battle between good and evil is merely the light and darkness of a soul's deeds.

A good act creates light, a bad act creates darkness, hence the term good and evil. It should be a perfectly good way of understanding the laws of Karma, that exist for all, no one can escape them. Every single bad deed has to be accounted for, every single good deed is accounted for. By your spiritual light are you known in the Kingdom of Heaven. By the darkness that surrounds you are you also known.

A person's energy field, often spoken of as the aura, never lies! Even every single illness that a person has had and is going to get is in the aura!

If doctors could read the aura around a person as well as we can in the spiritual Realms, what a difference it would make in the healing field! Everyone has an energy field around them, an aura is just another name for it.

The aura holds a great deal of information about the person it surrounds. It can tell if a person is well, or ill, if a disease is threatening or has just passed. It can tell if a person is kindly or not. It can also tell if a person has evil intentions or not!

If auras could be seen as clearly as I see them from my side of life, what a difference it would make on the earthplane. Criminals might think twice, and other nasty people who commit crimes such as murder and rape, must face the consequences when they eventually pass over into the darker Realms, called Hell by so many people.

It is always easier to ignore something that we do not want to do, or something that perhaps we do not want to accept. For example, if a soul living on the earthplane was aware of hearing voices from the spirit world, yet was afraid to either answer these voices, or even admit to oneself that these voices existed inside one's head, then just perhaps they may think that they are schizophrenic. However, this is by no means the case.

There is a very great difference between schizophrenia and hearing voices from the spirit Realms. An imbalance in the brain can cause schizophrenia, but this can be kept under control by medication. If a soul hearing voices was not schizophrenic, this can also be proven. The evidence and messages would no doubt astound them, as loved ones and many other spiritual beings speak of wondrous happenings, and give messages of comfort and joy. Also revealing an intimate knowledge of a person's lifestyle.

To be able to communicate with a loved one in the spiritual Realms, can have far reaching consequences for all concerned. It can and often does change a person's life and way of thinking. It even changes the way a person feels, because to have a sudden revelation that there is no death, only eternal life, is a major discovery to the person who first realises it.

Then the questions begin. Who are you? What do you want to say to me? Why are you coming to see me at all? Interest is aroused, and wow! When these questions are answered, usually in thought form, knowledge begins to flow in, often with a sense of awe and wonderment by the soul receiving the vital information. Knowledge is everyone's right. To take away knowledge under any circumstances is wrong. A crime against the laws of the Universe.

However, the truth is not always told by some who live in the spirit world. Sometimes mischief can get in and a soul can hear an awful lot of rubbish, things they long to happen, good things, surprises, etc. When these fail to materialize doubts begin to creep in, and once again the voyage of discovery begins.

Let us assume that a young man begins to make contact with the spirit world, by hearing a voice in his head speaking to him. He is told of wondrous things that will come to pass in his life, but they do not! It is all lies! So where is the information coming from?

I shall explain the art of mediumship so more people will understand exactly how it works.

In all worlds, the worlds of matter, and the many spirit levels of communication have good and bad, just like fruit, it is not always good. The bad fruit has to be picked out, just the same as the messages from the spirit world have to be tested and proven to be correct. Some people assume that every single thing they hear from the spirit world, is one hundred per cent correct, without even testing what they are given.

Let me put it another way, when a person hears a voice in their head from the spirit world, they should see or sense the vibration. If it feels loving and full of light, then it is a good message. However, if an uneasy feeling overcomes the person, or a sense of something not right, then the message is coming from a low vibration, or mischief maker, and the message is to be ignored and the spirit mischief maker is to be sent packing at once.

The best way to do this is to ask one's guide. Everyone has a guide to teach and help them to understand, and will answer questions that the person asks about. But questions of a nosy nature, or about someone else's private business, is never answered under any circumstances, because it is wrong. It is a law of the Universe, never to interfere in anyone else's private affairs.

When a guide is asked to help to remove the mischievous spirit from the person's auric field, which is often where communication takes place, he will do so. If not asked then he will not interfere, even though he is aware of all that is going on.

Until a person asks for help, no help can be given, for it is again interfering in another's business. But as soon as help is requested it is instantly given.

But how does one discover if one has drawn a mischievous spirit around them?

The tell-tale signs are when unwanted thoughts of an unkind, cruel or unpleasant nature start to pour into a person's head for no apparent reason, in between their own thoughts. They may feel aggressive towards someone they love, for no reason at all, feelings of hopelessness and inadequacy can frequently be felt.

There was once a very young girl who lived quite happily with her Mother and Father. Until one day she began to change, not dramatically, but slowly her personality began to change from a kind caring person. She began to be violent and had mood swings so often, no one knew where they were with her.

Then someone spotted how her eyes seemed to darken and change, and become so unlike her own, only momentarily during these violent outbursts.

There was one person who could see and hear all sorts of things from the spirit world, and knew exactly what was happening to the young girl. This person was a medium and knew that the young girl had a very nasty spirit drawn close to her. This nasty spirit had drawn so close to the child, he could inflict his own horrible feelings of anger so strongly into her auric field, and unhappily to say, the young girl responded.

She was always very sorry after a violent outburst, but could simply not understand why it had happened. Yet all the time these unpleasant incidents were going on she was aware of a very malicious old man who troubled her greatly.

She became aware of him at bedtime, and she often caught a glimpse of him out of the corner of her eye. She knew he was a bad man and she didn't like it one bit. But when she complained to her parents, they scoffed and said it was her imagination. How wrong they were!

The medium stepped in and the nasty spirit was removed, and

sent back to the dark Realms where he belonged. If the guide had been asked as soon as things began to get out of hand, then things would never have advanced to such an unpleasant state of affairs.

Prayer is the most powerful of all vibrations. By prayer, I mean when a soul quietly seeks for guidance with humility and sincerity, not word repeated over and over again without any real meaning, it is just a waste of time. That only adds to a person's confusion, and to other souls who just hear words repeated over and over again. It's a really odd way of doing things.

It's all so very simple. If you need help or guidance, then just ask for it quietly in your soul with love, knowing you will quite definitely be heard, and the desperate plea will most certainly be answered by a very spiritual soul indeed.

The prayer may seem to have gone unanswered, but prayer is always answered. It is seen as a sacred plea for help throughout the Universe, and reaches the highest levels of spiritual communication.

However, let me assure those that suddenly wonder, who the nasty spirit visitor was who attached himself to the lovely young girl's aura.

I will explain how the mischievous spirit was able to draw close to the young girl. It happened when she was taken ill. She was in a weakened state, and put into a hospital ward, where an old man of mean intent had recently died.

This old man did not go on towards the light, which he was unable to see. He had never believed that there was anything but death, no life existed after death in his eyes. He was a cruel man during his lifetime, and when he saw the young girl, he saw her innocence and wanted to corrupt her.

He stayed close to the young girl, he was not only an unpleasant character, but also a very lost soul who needed a great deal of help. He stayed with the young girl, making occasional trips to see his friends who still lived in the physical world and were also not of the light, but greedy, selfish and very unkind people indeed. They could not see him, and were totally unaware of the nasty old spirit of their former friend.

The nasty spirit saw the lovely young girl and he drew close, wishing that she could see him and be kind to him. He knew she had lovely thoughts, kind actions and always tried to do her best. When she cried, he cried, because the thoughts and feelings of both the nasty spirit and the young girl were mingled together.

He could not understand her wanting to help others. He had always destroyed what he could. He knew that he was doing wrong, but he wanted the young girl to do and act as he had during his earthly life. When he was finally removed by the spirit guide, the young girl at once became her old self again, full of joy, light and laughter, no more violent outbreaks or unspeakable acts of cruelty on all who tried to help her.

When the medium saw what was happening, she immediately requested help to remove the offensive spirit from the girl's auric field, and peace was restored.

This is a true story and happened not so long ago either. When a soul wishes to ask for help, or knowledge, or perhaps a selfish deed, or even asks to win a lot of money for selfish purposes, then it is answered! Not always the way perhaps it was thought it would be, but there is a law that runs throughout the Universe, the law of cause and effect.

A selfish prayer, will draw a selfish spirit to aid a request, and so on. A very spiritual request will also be answered on that level.

The laws of cause and effect are there for everyone, none can escape the law, for sooner or later it will affect every single living soul, so they might as well become aware of it, instead of blindly doing selfish and even barbaric acts of cruelty, thinking they can get away with it! They cannot, no one can!

CHAPTER FIVE

Self-Awareness

It is better to think ahead, rather than be a money-grabbing soul with no thought for others or the spiritual values of life.

On the earthplane there are still so many prisons, which are full to bursting point, like cauldrons ready to spill over, which on occasion they do. There does not seem to be the desired effect given to these criminals, which is to help them to a better understanding of all eternal life, and why they do what they do.

If the price they will have to one day pay was known to them, they would think twice about what they are doing.

When a highly evolved soul from my world chooses to help someone, perhaps by merely answering a cry for help from someone, regardless of the crimes they have committed during their life on the earthplane.

The highly evolved soul from the heavenly Realms, who will respond to the desperate plea for help and guidance, will never leave the person until his work is done and his services are no longer required.

Then gradually, kinder thoughts of love and upliftment will begin to filter through to the lost soul who has prayed for help. His or her life will then begin change for the better, and their thoughts will also improve, as they are gradually helped along their chosen life's pathway.

However, if an evil doer asks for help to do more evil, then a very corrupt soul may well be attracted to him, and add to the bad thoughts he or she already has. No one can assume that help of a most spiritual nature, will be given to someone who intends to do harm.

There are no lies that go undetected in my world. All is seen and known for what it truly is. The truth is always seen on all levels in the heavenly Realms.

The hospital wards are full of people who could be helped by spiritual guidance, combined with their recommended medication. For example, when a person suddenly experiences a shock of one kind, or another, then instantly a mental block is transferred to the emotional body, which in turn goes into the physical body creating disease, illness, and imbalance of the physical frame. To be able to go back to a certain incident that triggered off, perhaps, a whole chain of events, leading to a very serious illness for instance, can slowly begin to release the trauma. As realisation dawns when the first signs of disease begin to show in the physical body, there's a lot of things to be taken into consideration, but over all the mind plays a major part in maintaining good health.

Any imbalance created through trauma, can and will eventually effect the physical body of a soul upon the earthplane. To release this chain of events and restore the balance, would be to go back to the incidents one by one, and relive the experience all over again, then release the feelings that go with the incidents, for example, crying will help, shouting; suppressed anger can and does terrible things to the human body of someone on the earthplane.

However, it is not an easy life upon the earthplane, as I know only too well! Suffering often goes hand in hand with health. But wisdom which is a greater knowledge, can help to balance these symptoms that can occur from unhappy events that I have mentioned.

Homeopathy treats the whole person, but it is not always the answer, as the treatment can be quite harsh if one has suffered greatly during their lifetime. As the experiences which have caused the disease, or state of imbalance, as I like to refer to it, is released in much the same way as it happened.

It can be a very painful business, when one experiences the pain of a past trauma some years later, without any knowledge of it! But it is the best medicine on the earthplane that redresses the balance.

But a far better way is cause and effect, find out what caused the imbalance, and this can always be found in one's memory banks if they truly want to know, then action re-play with thoughts will eventually release the emotions that have created the imbalance, and slowly but gradually, health will be restored.

The mind is the key to all the information that one needs for perfect health. In certain situations, not all, some may be caused by Karma.

There are some karmic illnesses that there won't be a cure for, because the soul has chosen that specific experience for the duration of their life on the earthplane. But these are exceptional cases, and very hard lessons are learned.

However, the medical profession plays a very important part, and the earthplane would be in dire straits indeed without it.

A person in the physical body has unlimited resources. The human frame and mental body should work together in harmony, and when this does not happen, then it is natural for imbalances to occur.

Then it is up to the person involved to sort the matter out, by reflecting deeply on the cause of all their problems. Once this is done, then healing can take place.

But this is not always as easy as it sounds, and a cure does not usually happen overnight. It can be a long drawn out business of self-discovery, before healing takes place, and one is restored to good health.

It is also known that some imbalances are created through past life experiences, and these people who haven't dealt with a past life problem will have to deal with it in this life, or suffer the consequences.

This isn't as drastic as it sounds, because sometimes it is only a minor thing, and can be dealt with very quickly.

But there are certain people who are just too frightened to explore the reason why they are ill, and in these situations nothing can be done because it is their decision and should be respected. But there have been other situations were healing prayers have gone out, which is a very different thing altogether, and remarkable healing has taken place. Prayers are always answered.

I would like to tell you about a young lady who suffers dreadfully with her nerves. She is frightened to such an extent that she is mistrustful of everyone she meets. This was not always the case.

It all began about ten years ago, when something in her life triggered off the imbalance, which gradually got worse as time passed. Nothing the girl can do in the way of taking sleeping pills or tranquillizers will help to cure her nervous state. It may be pushed to the back of her mind. She may be lulled into a sense of false security with the medication she is constantly taking in the hope of effecting a cure.

If only she was to sit quietly and think back to when her nerves first began to get worse. Until gradually she is the neurotic, frightened person she has become.

She would find the reason for her bad nerves first stemmed from when she was a child and she got lost while on holiday with her family. For almost four hours she wandered about the busy seaside town crying and looking for her parents.

She was very frightened indeed, and when it grew dark and night fell, she was accosted by a man who only wanted to help her, but because he was dressed like a tramp and rather smelly, she was even more afraid and ran away down a very dark street.

It was during the night that she became worn out, and fell asleep on an old mattress that someone had flung onto a rubbish tip. She awoke as light was just beginning to break through. She was cold, tired and hungry, and absolutely terrified.

A milkman doing his rounds spotted her, and called out to her, asking if she was lost. He was a familiar sight, and she responded by going towards him, and admitting she was lost and very scared. The kindly milkman gave her a drink of milk, and a ride on his wagon to the nearest police station, where the child was soon recognised. Her parents had been beside themselves with worry, and were very relieved to know that their little daughter was safe and unharmed.

As time passed, she grew up into a very attractive young lady, but with such a nervous disorder that threatened to ruin her life. Her childhood experience was almost forgotten.

If someone had only asked if anything had happened in the past to upset and frighten her, and had she suffered from nightmares because of it? She would have replied that she had. Then a whole wave of pent up feelings of emotion would come flooding out and eventual release would automatically follow, until she was restored to a more balanced state and able to enjoy her life as never before, without the fear of the past trauma spoiling her life.

She also suffered asthma attacks on a regular basis; although mild they were still very frightening. There had also been another incident in the young girl's life that had led to her having breathing problems.

When she was a little baby, she had accidentally got locked in a very dark cupboard with little air, and the air was musty, which she hadn't like to breathe.

The experience didn't last long, perhaps an hour, but later in life epileptic fits began. So once again she should revert back to the unpleasant trauma, remembering every little unpleasant incident, especially the musty smell she hated so much.

Then gradually the asthma would go and normal breathing would follow in due course. It depends entirely on the person and how quickly they can deal with their problems on an emotional level.

It can be a very painful journey of self-discovery. But at the end of the road lies better health and a greater understanding of oneself. which is just another state of awareness. The return to a healthy state may take quite a long time.

However, this is not always the case. It has been known on occasion, that quite startling recoveries have occurred in a very short time indeed, once the reason for the illness is found.

Meditation is good for everyone, it's also good for the soul. The answers to all one's problems lies there, and it is the best form of communication between the mind and the soul. Also one can be greatly helped through prayer.

There are still so many people afraid to look at themselves, really look at how they feel, what they really want out of their life, and why they need all the things they think they need!

To know yourself inside out is a very wise state of affairs to be in. Self-knowledge of the Universe and of self is what it's all about. There are so many wondrous things to see and experience, and it's foolish not to know about them. To exist in a state of ignorance is of no use to anyone.

There still remains almost two thirds of the population of the earthplane that don't know or have the faintest idea why they are living their life. They are just plodding along in a very ignorant fashion, just enjoying the simple everyday things that occur in their lives.

If they were to receive a communication from a very spiritual source. They would probably choose to ignore it, and pretend it never happened, which is quite a common occurrence.

Then there are those other kind of people who do nothing but pray and hope that somebody might answer their prayers. But they never expect to get an answer, through a voice or thought in their head, for the solution to their problems. This may seem a little far fetched to some people, yet it is the absolute truth.

If more people became aware. Then all the needless suffering would not be necessary, because they would automatically know the reason why it happened, and how it came about. Perhaps through a chain of circumstances, sometimes very unhappy ones, which may have led to someone committing suicide, for instance.

There was once a young boy, almost eleven years old, and he was suffering intolerably from school bullying. His parents, however, were totally unaware of the boy's misery and frightened countenance. They were so wrapped up in their own selfish pleasures that they failed to notice how often he locked himself away in his room. They knew nothing of his despair. Yet he lived in the same house as them, ate at the same table as them, and still they remained totally ignorant to the true state of affairs that existed between them and their son.

If only they had been more aware, more caring, then they would have instantly known that something was very, very wrong.

The young boy, with a wonderful life ahead of him, committed suicide by hanging from the neck in an old school barn, not far from where he lived.

His parents were naturally devastated when they were told about their son's death. They suddenly remembered all the little signs of unhappiness he had portrayed during his young and very unhappy life.

It was all so needless, all such a waste of a young boy's life. His cry for help went unheard upon the earthplane, but it was most assuredly heard in the heavenly Realms, where I exist. But the young boy was so wrapped up in his own pain and misery that he listened to no one from our side of life.

When he eventually died, we were there to receive him into our loving arms. How he cried and sobbed when he discovered what he had done.

All the pain and misery flooded over him. Then was soon washed away by the very beautiful and soothing feelings of peace all around him.

He lay in a very serene and tranquil atmosphere, where healing was taking place within the young boy's mind. He realised that the choice he had made, had been the only way out of his very painful and desperate plight at that time of his evolvement. But now in the peaceful rays of the healing centre, which is where he was taken to, he began to realise that he had been foolish, and it was just another very harsh lesson upon the earthplane that he had to learn.

No one ever criticized him or took him to task for ending his own life. He was treated with the utmost kindness and love, and responded so well that his recovery was quite quick.

He began to ask all sorts of questions of his guide, and wanted to see everything immediately! So eager was the little chap to learn about the heavenly Realms.

There are many people of the opinion that to take one's life is a sin in the eyes of God. In my eyes the greater sin is that a soul should feel so desperately lonely and frightened in the first place, and the only course of action left to them is to end their life is very sad indeed.

At sometime in their other physical lives, should they choose to be born into the earthplane again, they will have to re-learn the lesson which is to overcome all obstacles with faith and love, such is God's law.

It is no easy task, trying to show kindness and compassion to those who are unkind or try to harm someone. But in time, they too will learn the many lessons that lead to spirituality. It is the soul's growth.

CHAPTER SIX

Lost Worlds

A soul can experience great hardship during an earthly life. It was a great relief to me when my life was over, and I didn't need to re-live another physical life experience. Because there was nothing left for me to learn.

I now reside in the Realms of Heaven in a very supreme state of bliss. But it is not an idle existence by any means, because I also try to help others.

In fact, I belong to a group of very spiritual souls indeed, who do their utmost to help others. And our greatest desire is to bring peace and harmony to the earthplane, as it was in the past.

There was a time, many centuries ago, when space beings were regular visitors to the island of Lemuria. They were highly evolved spiritual beings, who flew through the galaxies in their space ships on missions of research.

They were well over seven feet in height, with very long arms and legs. Their fingers and toes were short and stumpy, and they had suction pads on the surface of their hands and feet for holding things.

Their skin tone was of a crinkly texture, and off white in colour. They also had rather small mouths which they used for eating purposes. They didn't need to communicate via the mouth, because they had reached a stage in their evolution, when they communicated by thought waves.

These highly evolved space beings harmed no one, and indeed

helped many other souls they came into contact with on their various trips around the galaxies. The Mu people were well known by these space visitors, and an alliance was struck between the Mu people and the planet in the solar system that they came from.

It was common knowledge to the people on the island of Lemuria, who were a very clever race of people indeed, almost like super beings with great powers, There were many great scientists among them.

It was a time long before Atlantis even existed. These people mapped out the stars and knew of other planets in the solar system were different life forms also existed.

They were always pleased to receive any help from their regular space visitors, who were seen constantly. They did not fear them, because they knew they were highly evolved, spiritual beings, and would not harm them.

However, it all came to rather an abrupt end, when an explosion of nuclear energy blew up the earthplane, as it was then, and destroyed all life on the island of Lemuria. The contract was forgotten between the Mu people and their space friends that no weapons of any description should ever be made or used. This was the law.

The explosion was all their own fault. When they discovered the nuclear energy they just had to test it and blew everyone and everything to smithereens.

I was part of that life on the Isle of Mu, as it was called then. That was a very long time ago. Yet, even today, man on the earthplane is testing nuclear warfare, which is a very dangerous thing to do. If they are not careful they will destroy their own planet!

There was also a time when man destroyed another civilisation, the city of Atlantis, by nuclear energy. If they had only stopped to realise that their actions would not only kill every living thing on their planet, but also the shock waves could be felt by those in the air living in other dimensions.

It was felt in every other vibrational field as a very great evil deed upon all life that existed on and around the city of Atlantis. This is common knowledge to quite a few people on the earthplane, and has had far reaching consequences for many souls who have incarnated since then. Their responsibility is to restore the damage that they did in that life. In fact, their Karma has brought them into a life situation where they can choose to do only good things during their lives on the earthplane.

These people are often in a place of power, able to command certain things of other people, and their orders are carried out to the letter. Great responsibility is not an easy task. Therefore, it should be with great consideration and thought for the benefit of all mankind that these actions should be of the highest order. Unfortunately, this is not always the case.

There is still fighting going on at the very moment I am writing, man is killing man, and what is it all for? Equal rights?

I don't think so. There has never been a time when fighting was the right thing to do, no matter what the provocation might be. Although, I hasten to add, there have been times when one has had to defend oneself, but that is quite a different matter altogether. Slavery was one crime against man. The killing of Jesus was another.

The atrocities that are committed upon the earthplane for no apparent reason, often fill me me with horror at the lack of understanding that still persists, even after all this time. Man's inhumanity to man is still going on in the most dreadful situations.

If these people were to stop and think of the cause and effect of their actions, they might try to repair any damage they had done and lead a more spiritual life.

It isn't an easy life to live on the earthplane, but live and learn is the motto. Until the time comes when all will understand, fighting and cruelty will be paid for in every situation.

For example, I will tell you the true story of a young man who went off to war. He didn't want to fight the so-called enemy, but he had little choice in the matter. He was sent abroad on active service with his regiment.

Then the mass killing and slaughter began, all in the name of God. As so many prayed, there were no chosen few, God heard all their prayers and tried to stop the killing, but man would not listen. All, except one, ignored the inner voice of reason.

The young man listened to all he was told about killing his enemy, and he was in a quandary as to what he should do. If he should just walk away from the battlefield, he would be called a traitor and a coward and shot. He didn't want to leave in that manner, but he didn't want to kill anyone either.

The matter was taken out of his hands when he was blown to bits by a mortar shell. It landed a direct hit on him and he shot into the heavenly Realms. A world full of peace. His prayers had been answered, and he was very glad indeed to be out of the situation.

That has happened many times when a poor soul has prayed to God to help him, and to take him away from the mass killing and needless slaughter that is going on all around him.

It is an act of divine providence, because the desire for peace is so great within a person's soul, they trigger off certain vibrations that can have far reaching consequences. Because everyone has a certain energy field which is all their own, rather like their name.

In these instances, a frequency of energy goes out and is picked up by someone not on the earthplane. This is how it works, when a soul is seriously injured in the line of battle. Their vibration changes dramatically and they are aware that they are going to die. They should be glad that their earthly life and suffering is over and they are able to return to a better place. A much wiser soul for all the knowledge they had acquired during their life on the earthplane. Instead of perhaps feeling a sense of great terror at passing over into the unknown, which is nothing at all. It is the suffering that accompanies death that is where the fear should lie, not the actual state of death itself.

However, there are some people who realise that death is but the parting from one world to enter another in the spirit world. There should be no fear of death, it is merely the most natural thing in the Universe, for all matter changes constantly. Birth and death, not of the soul for that can never die, but of the physical body, is as natural as all the colours in the Universe.

It is a grand thing to be able to look towards the death of the physical body with a knowledge that they will be released and set free for another learning experience. Perhaps even on another planet!

I have learnt a very great deal during my many lifetimes, and there is so much more to learn. For the Universe is vast and filled with boundless mysteries that one can discover. And I have all the time in the world. In fact, I have all eternity!

Astral travel is another way of learning about the Universe, and everyone has the natural ability to astral travel. It is as easy as falling off a log! But not always so easy to remember, which matters not at all, because the soul will remember. When the soul flies free during sleep state, it can be a truly wonderful experience for all concerned.

A soul takes many journeys and voyages of discovery, before finding a spiritual peace within, and knows that their faults have all gone with the passage of time.

To suddenly realise that one has evolved to such a state of consciousness that they can now ascend even higher, and begin to be even more spiritual than before. However, in some situations it can be a very complicated business, as the soul may try many times to overcome obstacles along the way before any progress can be made. But in time they too will learn.

The ability to learn and grow in wisdom and knowledge is what it is all about. Why be afraid and ignorant of the laws of the Universe? Why shut down one's memory banks and refuse to accept all that exists because it can't be seen with the physical eyes? And to close the mind firmly against any psychic knowledge from creeping in, is foolish to say the least!

There is one Universal Law for all life, not only on the earthplane, but also throughout the galaxies where thought prevails.

That is love one another. Love is the key to all spiritual knowledge and wisdom. The desire to learn for selfish reasons, most definitely will not attract a highly evolved spiritual being of the light.

There have been life forms since the planet earth first began to cool down, even before the first tiny speck of life could be born, there was life beyond the stars.

There are life forms in many dimensions, and some are so advanced they can orbit the sun and moon and not be any older. For there is no time in the Universe. To these space beings it is an accepted practice to travel in this way.

There are life forms beneath the sea that still exist in a dimension beyond time and space, and they are not fish! They are often referred to as extraterrestrials. They exist in water and travel far and wide beneath the many oceans on the earthplane.

They have been aware of ships lost at sea and have tried to help on many occasions, but all to no avail, because they exist in another time scale. This does not mean that they are not aware of what is going on in another dimension. Their only reason for existing beneath the sea is to learn about water and tidal waves, and how the moon and stars interact with the ocean. They can only exist for a very short time out of the water on dry land. But this is not their way. They live quite happily beneath the oceans of the earthplane.

There are also space creatures of super intelligence who can exist almost anywhere in the Universe. They are indeed Godlike creatures, for their light is very bright indeed. These creatures are very well thought of and respected on many levels, by many other individuals in outer space belonging to different dimensions. Space travel is only a matter of time to some beings. To others it is a matter of fact.

I might add, that space ships have frequently been seen by people on the earthplane, yet, it is still shrouded in deep mystery and suspicion. Do you really think that a spaceling who has greater knowledge and knows how to travel faster than the speed of light, would really want to harm another living soul, much less a human being on planet earth?

There is still so much more to learn. The Universe and all its secrets are there to be explored, and it's there for everyone to explore, either in this lifetime or another. You choose whether to limit yourself or not! No one can tell you how to go about it. You already know great things that are buried deep in the subconscious.

The secret doorway to extraterrestrial knowledge, and also to one's own spiritual growth, lies within. To grow in knowledge and wisdom is everyone's destiny.

A very long time ago, before man began to exist upon the planet earth, certain changes had to come about.

These changes enabled many visits from beings from other planets, to come on exploration trips and examine the atmosphere and the ground. Samples were taken for tests, and it was found that the ground would be very good to grow vegetation on.

It was in fact ideal as an organic garden. A variety of plants were planted from other planets and left to grow. In time these plants became trees and forests, and lovely flowers grew. Until the earthplane was filled from one end to the other with lush green vegetation, suitable for consumption by the many small creatures and still tiny animals that lived there amongst all the foliage.

It was still quite hot in certain areas of the earthplane. However, the cooling down system had began within the earth's atmosphere. Then began the gradual process of growth by certain animals. In fact, their size was enormous which is well documented, even films have been made about these prehistoric creatures that lived on land and sea.

This was a very slow evolution, until the species became more intelligent and life became more difficult, because man began to evolve slowly, but surely.

The early ape man began to seek for his own, things that did not belong to him. All peace suddenly began to take on a different aspect as man began to hunt and kill animals to survive as meat eaters. This was totally unnecessary, as man does not need meat to survive.

As time went by, however, things began to change, and life on the planet earth has evolved up to present day in the year 1997.

However, during the evolution of man upon the planet earth, there were other souls who watched over these proceedings and monitored everything that was going on between man and the planet.

The onlookers were aghast at man's inhumanity to man, and it was decided to leave the planet earth to its own devices, and these space brothers withdrew to their own galaxy far away in the

Universe. But they still kept an eye on it from a distance, by listening to energy vibrations, and telepathic communication was also used. This is an excellent way of learning what is going on.

But that was long ago, and it is common knowledge to almost everyone on the earthplane what occurred during the dinosaur age. But not many people are aware of the help and guidance they received from other more spiritual and enlightened souls from other planets. Space ships haven't suddenly popped up, they have been visiting the earthplane since before anyone even existed there!

There are different lifestyles on different planets throughout the solar system. All are friendly, except one life form from a planet nearer to the moon. It is not a popular place to visit, as there is great danger and negativity on that planet. But no one goes there anyway, and they are not able to travel far in time or space.

To visit this planet is asking for trouble because they are such a negative race of beings. Their world is indeed a dark and gloomy place to live in. However, this does not concern anyone else, the information is given to enlighten you.

There are many alien life forms in the Universe, and there is one above all others who are extremely spiritual and will help anyone in need.

These space brothers first became known in Egypt, when their flying ships were a regular sight to many. Although not everyone had the ability to see them, because of the density of the air upon the earthplane. But others could see them quite clearly, and were unafraid, knowing that they came with great love for all mankind.

The Egyptians were a cruel and barbaric race. They were great builders, regardless of the suffering it entailed, life wasn't held at all sacred in those days. When someone in authority died, all their servants were entombed alive with them, no concern for their suffering was ever shown by those who did this terrible thing. But it was common knowledge that their Gods wanted it this way. It was supposed to help them into the next world.

However, many a cruel person has only arrived in the darker Realms, because of his thoughts and unkindly deeds, and to find himself devoid of any servants or riches. This is always a great shock to them.

But the poor suffocated alive servants have found themselves in a place of such wondrous beauty that they have grown fearful in case it was a trap! So great had their fear and humiliation been during their earthly lives, when no kindness had ever been shown to them.

They soon recovered, and tears of joy were to be seen as the truth was gently explained to them.

The law of the Universe is not to harm anyone, but to love one another and to help in any way that one can. The space brothers have been doing this for a very long time. Their life span is far longer than the physical body is on the earthplane. Centuries have passed, and still there is so much lack of knowledge on the earthplane.

Nevertheless, this knowledge is accepted and understood by many lifeforms throughout the Universe. But on the earthplane many of these facts are still a mystery. It is fear of the unknown that holds people back, and these feelings of negativity are easily picked up by others in the solar system, rather like a letter reaches its destination on the earthplane, it's communication of a kind. Fear stops progress of the soul and one's emotional progress.

Fear is a very real thing and it's to be overcome in all areas of mankind. Fear is the closed door to knowledge and can hold a soul back from all sorts of things. Fear will eventually kill a soul in a physical body, and is paramount to suicide, find the reason behind the fear and release it.

When the fear has gone, a soul then begins to expand in truth and knowledge, which is what a physical life is all about.

CHAPTER SEVEN

The Search for Truth

There are many more interesting things in the Universe that I should like tell you about. For instance, it is quite widely known that meteorites exist and can, and often do go hurtling through space, sometimes barely missing a planet on its downward descent. At other times it has landed smack bang in the middle of a planet and destroyed it completely. However, at other times it has also merely whizzed by, and only the vibrations are felt on a planet when this happens.

There is shortly to be due another comet of immense size that will almost touch the planet earth, but no harm will befall anyone.

It will merely send shock waves throughout the globe. All these are harmless but quite unpleasant when first felt.

The shock waves are quite severe in certain areas. But still no damage shall be done at any time during the meteorite's headlong flight.

I should also like to add that these things have been predicted many times throughout earth's history. I would also like to say that the meteorite will be closely followed by a space ship of immense size, and can be seen by certain people, others will see nothing. It is all a matter of wavelengths and evolution of a person's soul.

There is a vast and huge expanse of space still unchartered by many spirit brothers. They send out what I shall call scouts, to explore certain nether regions to see if the possibility of life still exists.

It is a wondrous thing to be able to explore the heavens, to have the knowledge that there is life outside one's own domain. Life exists, as I know only too well!

There is also another life form that I have not mentioned. It is the smaller species who are approximately three feet high.

They are often called the greys by some people on the earthplane. These greys are not malicious or unkind in any way at all, but they do like to visit the earthplane at regular intervals, for their experiments on human life!

These greys, that is not their real name, call themselves the visitors, as they are always visiting different planets on their voyage of discoveries. Their planet is out of sight of the earthplane. It exists beyond the planet Jupiter

It is a very long way off by some standards on the earthplane, but not to our kindly little visitors. They have been known to beam up certain people of the human race, but they have never harmed anyone at all.

In fact, they like to communicate by sending thought waves out, and waiting to see if they get an answer from people who are not afraid on the earthplane.

The people that say they are alien abductions are quite genuine, but what they don't realise is that they themselves have agreed by prior arrangement, perhaps when they looked up at the stars and said, 'I would like to see someone from another planet!'

The thought is very quickly picked up by the little visitors. There have sometimes been a great many messages wishing to meet them!

There will be even more people in the future of the earthplane able to see our little visitors. They will also see advanced souls from other dimensions.

All kindly and all with good intentions, but none will interfere in anybody's spiritual growth, or their free will under any circumstances.

This is the law of the Universe that is strictly kept to, and none will break it, for they have simply gone beyond the thought of interference. They have no desire to harm anyone. Indeed they are quite chatty and very friendly.

It has been discussed in the past, where someone has memories of being aboard a space ship, or of losing time for no reason that they can think of; all this is quite true.

Time on the earthplane is of no value, or of importance to space brothers who do not work by the clock, not a clock on the earthplane anyway! They mean no harm and to my knowledge, which is vast, they have never harmed anyone at all.

However, there is another kind of space visitor who perhaps is not so kindly, because they are devoid of all emotion, rather like a robot! These space brothers are not very intelligent by the standards of other spacelings. They are not well liked at all, yet, no one ever lifts a finger to harm them, because they will learn how wrong it is to harm another creature, even one in a different dimension.

These spacelings are also grey with slanting almond eyes which are jet black. They are taller than our kindly visitors, but very similar in stature. The only difference is that they do not give off any kindness, because that is an emotion to make one smile.

They are not intentionally evil, because they do not know the meaning of the word. However, they can do some very unkind things to themselves, which causes harm and creates a feeling of pain which they do not like.

There are many of these little visitors flying about the Universe, and hopefully in time, they will learn to be of a lighter frequency filled with spiritual growth.

When these creatures are seen on the earthplane, which is still a very rare occurrence, they are instantly on their guard, and can disappear at will into their own vibration. They can only look at human beings on the earthplane. They can't touch, harm or beam anyone up into their ship. They simply watch and hopefully learn as they travel the galaxies.

They have no wish to harm anyone. It's because they can't feel things in quite the same way as someone who is more spiritually evolved. But hopefully they will grow in wisdom and knowledge as time passes. They can communicate with each other, but not in a language anyone on the earthplane would understand.

The search for truth and knowledge is a difficult one. Because people are still afraid to accept the truth for fear of ridicule, they even ignore their own senses when they are told, or shown, that life after death exists.

On the earthplane it is well known that there are still people who don't believe in life after death of the physical body. They prefer to go on believing that the only life there is, is the one they are living. Loneliness is a terrible affliction that affects the soul. To be able to walk alone, knowing that life exists throughout the galaxies is a wondrous thing that brings peace and tranquillity.

After all, no one was born with someone special beside them, and no one will die with their special love at exactly the same instant, and go on to the exact same place in the Realms of Heaven. This is just not possible.

Loneliness is lack of understanding and lack of communication of the soul. Most people yearn for love and friendship at some time in their lives this is natural, but the fear of being alone is not.

When a soul is bereft of a loved one that they have shared most of their earthly life with, a feeling of such desolation often overwhelms them, as they begin to realise that they are alone, perhaps for the first time in their lives. Their loved one has merely returned home to the spirit world, which is where everyone truly belongs, for a short duration.

The new arrival will be taken to a healing sanctuary, filled with divine feelings of peace and tranquillity, where healing takes place, and the painful memories of their passing will fade into insignificance. It is the soul left behind who is still suffering.

It isn't an easy life on the earthplane, suffering goes hand in hand with joy, many times during an earthly life. And losing a loved one is one of the hardest lessons of all.

When a soul knows that their loved one will be there to greet them when their time comes to pass over, it often helps them to cope with the sense of loss, and gives them an inner strength to go on.

There have been many times throughout the history of the human race, when man has doubted that life after death exists. But in time everyone will come to know the truth.

The soul is something unseen, but most assuredly exists. It's the life force of all living things. It's the soul's journey of evolution that is the meaning of all life. It's all part of the divine plan.

Survival isn't the issue as many souls inhabit many bodies, usually in a physical body, until the lessons are learned. Then they pass away into the heavenly Realms.

When they are ready to try another life of learning, and this is not forced upon anyone, each soul makes their own decision, whether to have another life on the earthplane in a physical body, or to try something else!

The decision is entirely their own choice, no interference from anyone is ever permitted. They must make their own choice without hindrance of any kind from anyone.

However, plenty of help is given. They are shown pictures of scenes from different places that perhaps they are thinking of trying. They are also shown pictures of different lifestyles, to help them with their choice.

Let us assume that a soul who resides in the heavenly Realms, wishes to have another life experience upon the earthplane. He will have to choose the place, the era, and the precise time he wishes to be born. He will also choose his parents and friends that will be able to help him with whatever he feels he needs to experience.

Once the decision is made, the young soul, for he still has much to learn, although he has already sampled many lifetimes, is eager to begin another. When the time comes for him to be born, he has a rough idea of certain things he must do and things he should avoid during his lifetime on the earthplane. He must also decide whether to marry and have children or not!

All this is arranged before he is born into the earthplane. But not exactly to plan, more like rough guide lines, because free will plays a most important part in a soul's evolution. Spiritual growth is what it's all about.

The young soul has decided he would like to be born in London in the year 1886. He chooses his family, and permission is given by his parents to be, who are already married and living happily together on the earthplane.

They long for a lovely little baby and pray most earnestly that this should happen, and happen it most certainly does! Their prayer which is thought in action is heard in the heavenly Realms, and the young soul meets his parents to be when they are fast asleep in bed. Their souls travel to the lower planes of existence, often referred to as the lower astral. A meeting takes place and a pact is made.

When the young couple wake up all they can remember is snippets of a rather strange dream, they remember someone saying that they would have a little baby quite soon now. It's not important to remember anything for the soul knows!

The pregnancy takes the natural course of events, and a baby son is born to the young couple, who are absolutely delighted. He is greatly loved throughout his childhood and cared for to the best of their ability.

As the years pass, they become quite old, and soon they will pass over into the heavenly Realms. It will be a very sad time for their son, who has grown up into a very nice and kindly young man, due also to his upbringing.

He is not aware of being psychic, or at all interested in spiritual matters, but scoffs and ridicules them, as a lot of young men do!

Then his Father passes away quickly, and within a space of a few weeks, his dear Mother also passes away. The young man is devastated, and feels so alone and is terrified of the future. Yet, he becomes aware of a certain change in the air as he thinks of it.

He begins to get glimpses of his Father's face, and then sees his Mother's face. She is smiling at him. He hears her speak to him in his head, thoughts of love are showered on him, and he begins to understand that they're trying to tell him that they are not dead and they still love him dearly, and will always help him in any way that they can.

The young man feels a great sense of relief and also awe at what he has discovered. He suddenly becomes extremely interested in matters to do with life after death, and all other subjects to do with the psychic.

As his search for the truth that life is eternal begins, he makes many discoveries. To his great astonishment he finds he has a guide who is there to help him.

The guide and the young man have walked hand in hand during another lifetime, and when the guide in the heavenly Realms offered his help, the young man was very pleased to accept. The pathway to knowledge began for the young man and he learnt many things about life after death, taught to him by his guide.

It was a hard life he had chosen as a gamekeeper. He tramped miles over the countryside, and spent long hours out in all weathers, working for a very rich family indeed. He never married, this had been his choice before birth. The experience of being alone without feeling lonely had been his desire. But there were many times when he longed for a dear friend to share his life with, but he had not chosen it, so it did not happen.

It is very rare that a marriage takes place if it is not preordained, but because of free will, has been known to happen, and has to my knowledge not ended in happy circumstances. The choice to experience marriage is also a very painful or beautiful lesson, depending on the lesson the soul wishes to learn.

The young man had many friends, some even discussed spiritual matters with him, but none had learned as much as he had. He preferred his own company and the company of his guide on many occasions. He saw cruelty and neglect all around him. He saw poverty that made him want to cry. He wanted to help everyone he could, but he was a poor man, unlike the gentry who had plenty of money and not only held onto it, but spent nothing in helping anyone else! The greed for money is an empty thing.

The young man became quite old when he finally passed over into the heavenly Realms.

It was a very painful death, at his request. He had also chosen the way he wanted to die! When he eventually found himself back in the heavenly Realms, his joy knew no bounds. He met his parents and all his friends whom he had met during his earthly life. His guide was also there to greet him on his return. It was a very happy time indeed.

The young man re-lived the experiences of his earthly life in his mind, as pictures flashed before him. He saw all his faults and all his good deeds, and the mistakes that he knew he couldn't help at the time. He was shown all the good times and all the sad times. He knew he couldn't have done any better, because he had always tried to do his best. It was a great revelation to him and he knew that he had learned a very great deal.

He decided to stay where he was for a while, then perhaps when he was ready, he might like to help others in the astral world. He knew there was much work to do and many things to learn.

He also decided that when he was ready, he would like to try another life on the earthplane. But in the meantime, he wanted to go into a lower vibration and help those in need.

In time the young man experienced many lifetimes and learnt much. But the most important thing he learned, was to show love and kindness to all life forms throughout the Universe.

Love is the highest vibration that leads to perfection which is everyone's destiny.

CHAPTER EIGHT

When The Soul Flies Free

It is for the benefit of all mankind that these things are written about. To learn is to grow in peace and harmony, until such a time the lessons are all learnt and there is no necessity to go over the same thing again. When one has learnt a very hard lesson, they are very unwilling to go down the same pathway, even for someone they love.

There are many obstacles to overcome on life's pathway, so many painful situations to experience and many hardships to endure. But there is also the lighter side of life upon the earthplane. There is the joy of living, the peace of understanding, and the shining example one can become to others.

Once the experience is over and the lesson from it has been learnt, then it's always time to move on to other things. This is the way with all life forms.

For example, a lovely young woman is in despair in a very unhappy situation. She feels trapped and doesn't know what to do, but her soul knows the answer, and she must listen if she is to progress on her spiritual pathway. When someone is in extreme distress it effects the physical body, and in time their state of health will deteriorate.

When the decision has been made to move on, then it should be done as kindly and as gently as possibly, where other people are concerned. When the truth dawns on a soul that a life of freedom lies ahead, it's like watching a lovely flower come into full bloom.

It's no good trying to persuade anyone to stay in a crisis that is making them ill.

In the new life of rest, peace and harmony that has taken a long time to achieve, the young woman begins to find that she is sleeping better and her appetite has been restored. In fact, she is now enjoying life as never before. Thoughts of the past occasionally creep in, but the knowledge that she had done her best, leave her with no sense of guilt. After the healing period takes place, then it's time to go into the next experience, which need not be an unhappy one.

The joy of loving someone and being able to help them in many ways is also a blessing, but it can lead to many misunderstandings along the way. This is perhaps when the lesson of tolerance and compassion is learnt.

There are many experiences in a loving relationship, and not all are happy ones, some can be very painful lessons. It can be a very rewarding process in terms of suffering and spiritual evolvement.

There are many diseases on the earthplane that are triggered off by very unhappy circumstances. Stress is a major contributing factor in many an illness.

However, there are also many that are karmic, and many other illnesses that can be avoided if dealt with by the mind and emotional body at the same time. But frequently the mind realizes what has happened in a certain situation and does not feel it in the physical body, because it is suppressed. This can lead to a whole variety of minor complaints leading to sometimes quite major illnesses. A lot depends on a person's state of mind at the time of the blow or shock, or even a very unpleasant incident that happened years ago, that they can't remember.

For example, bruises that come out on the surface of the skin can be seen, but what about the bruises that go inside the physical body, the invisible ones! These are the bruises that often need help to heal. These are the trigger points for illnesses in many cases. But not all illnesses start with an accident or unhappy situations, sometimes it is merely the person themself who creates an illness.

For instance, let us assume that a woman in her late forties suddenly begins to feel very bitter, because she has never married or had children, simply because the opportunity didn't come her way. And there will be a deeper meaning behind that as well.

The woman eventually becomes even more bitter in her mind. As her resentment builds up, and she is unaware of the imbalances she is beginning to create within her physical body, she begins to feel unwell, and starts to visit the Doctor's surgery on a regular basis with one minor ailment after another.

She has constant attacks of migraine that she never previously suffered from. Her bowels begin to trouble her, and she daren't go very far because of the necessity to stay close to a toilet. She begins to lose sleep and also her joints begin to ache. A thing she has never experienced before.

As things go from bad to worse, and don't forget, the poor lady herself is creating the imbalance in her own physical body, the symptoms gradually get worse.

As the years fly by and she remains single and lives alone, her bitterness leads to self-pity, which aggravates her already very painful symptoms. In due course, she becomes very ill and eventually dies! This is the course all illnesses will take, if the state of the mind and physical body isn't taken care of.

One other instance that happened only a few years ago to a happy young man in his early thirties, was when his wife died suddenly, and he found himself unable to cope with the two children left behind and which he was responsible for.

He very gradually began to sink into a decline, drinking a great deal of alcohol and eating little. He began to take pills to help him sleep, and pills to aid him to keep alert throughout the day. Until eventually his health began to deteriorate, due to his situation that he felt he couldn't cope with. He soon became very ill and also died, leaving two small children without a Mother or Father to look after them. The trauma that the children experienced during their sad loss, resulted in them being taken care of in a very happy environment, with foster parents, of the highest standards.

However, the children's experiences would not effect them, until perhaps later in life. One child had a very nervous fear of death, which related to the loss of both parents and hadn't been dealt with properly. The other child had a great fear of insecurity, which carried on throughout his life for the very same reason. That it hadn't been dealt with.

It's the incidences in one's life that can create great happiness, joy, and peace of mind, and of course good health. But if one has suffered a great deal of turmoil in their life, as many people have, then it will reveal itself in the physical body, in time, if not dealt with.

As each soul is different, so the same incident that happens in exactly the same manner, as with the two children, will effect that person in a very different way, according to how they felt it at the time.

There are many illnesses created through past traumas that have happened in people's lives. The self-healing process begins and ends with a person's thoughts, which are of paramount importance, concerning their physical health. To maintain a healthy body, one must have a healthy mind. Fear alone can trigger off all sorts of things in the physical body, get rid of the reason for the fear, and the physical body will respond accordingly.

Some mental and physical disabilities are Karmic and therefore can't be healed. It's what the soul has chosen to go through before being born onto the earthplane, to gain knowledge from the experience. These are very brave souls indeed.

For there are many hard lessons involved in that learning experience. So next time you see someone who is disabled, be kindly in your thoughts towards them!

However, there is always someone to look after them, and that is their chosen pathway, to care for others who are unable to manage on their own, because of their illness. There are many Alzheimer sufferers on the earthplane, who will eventually lose all sense of reality with the world they are living in, until only the shell remains. At this stage there is very little, if any, form of communication. And it is difficult to understand what can be gained from this Karmic experience.

-It's the carers who look after these poor souls who suffer the most. It's not an easy task, in fact in many cases it's heartbreaking to watch a loved one losing their mental ability to communicate. They usually require around the clock attention.

Sometimes feelings of guilt can creep in, when the carer feels that they simply can't cope any more with the situation. This is natural and to be expected. The only choice left to them is to place their loved one in care.

There are very caring people on the earthplane, who actually enjoy looking after sick people, regardless of the illness. That also is their Karmic choice, and these are very spiritual souls indeed.

However, when a person abuses someone, they will in turn be abused, because this is the law of cause and effect.

Caring for an Alzheimer sufferer is one of the hardest lessons there is on the earthplane. It is indeed a labour of love. But where has the soul of an Alzheimer sufferer gone? Well, I shall tell you exactly what happens. As the brain cells die away and the mind becomes detached from reality, there is no recognition, no reality of their situation and no communication. In fact, there is only the body to be attended to, which is a very bleak prospect indeed for a carer. To lose a loved one in this way is a very painful business, so what is the lesson to be learned?

When a soul chooses to take on the burden of Alzheimer's disease, it has far reaching consequences for all concerned. It's not an isolated decision. An agreement before reincarnation takes place, and is agreed upon by others, who also wish to experience looking after Alzheimer sufferers.

However, it does not always go exactly according to plan, because everyone has the ability to change their mind about something! This is what free will is all about. Things can change, and even alter drastically, when a person changes their pathway of learning. This isn't wrong, only interesting, as other lessons are also learned. No one is a puppet! Everyone's emotions and feelings are different, so everyone reacts differently to a similar situation.

When a person suffers from Alzheimer's disease, their soul often leaves the physical body to wander about in another dimension, often referred to as the astral world, but I prefer to call it the spirit world, because that is exactly what it is. In actual fact, all they do is the same as most other people do when asleep. This is more commonplace than people think.

Margaret Clark has a Mother with Alzheimer's disease, and Margaret is aware that her Mum takes many journeys into the spirit world. She has in fact seen her Mother's spirit leave the body and also return to it many times. This frequently happens with most Alzheimer cases.

The precise time of death is also preordained before birth, and is a welcome release for many with an Alzheimer condition. But this doesn't necessarily happen at the exact time it was previously arranged, because of a person's free will, which as I have already stated, can change things. I call this taking a turn in the road. When this happens, a whole new set of situations appear, and different lessons are experienced to those previously expected on the life plan of a soul's journey.

When a soul chooses to be born into a physical body, they have no memory of why they are there, or what they are supposed to learn. But eventually they will return to the pathway they had chosen before their birth, nothing is wasted, new experiences never are. But it alters the time scale regarding a person's passing.

This sometimes makes a person want to try another life in the physical body, because of all the strange twists and turns their previous life took, until finally, there is nothing else they can learn in a physical body on the earthplane. Therefore, they will not feel the need to re-live anymore lives. Their physical incarnations are over and it's time to experience other things, perhaps on other planets! The choice is theirs to make and no one should interfere!

CHAPTER NINE

Past Life Memories

The Universe is vast and filled with all kinds of different life forms, each with its own frequency and wavelength of power. And on a communication level, much can be learned and passed down through the generations to come throughout the solar system, including on the earthplane.

To doubt that other life forms exist is to doubt the very existence of the stars!

I am now going to tell you about a soul's journey. This soul once lived a life upon the earthplane, and when his body was old and worn out he returned to the heavenly Realms, He was a very spiritual soul indeed.

After some time had passed in the spirit Realms, he decided that he would like to learn more about life on other planets.

During his life on the earthplane, he had spent most of his time looking up at the stars, wondering if life really did exist out there in the Universe. Then one day, he became aware that communication was taking place with other life forms, through telepathic communication.

Thoughts that he knew were not his own, but came from another intelligence, began to answer his many questions that he also asked in his mind, and each time a question was answered, he asked another one. Astounding predictions of future happenings that he was told about, also proved to be true.

He was aware that these beings had great knowledge that was far beyond his own. And he was considered to be extremely clever, with all the scientific background that made him quite an authority on aerospace dynamics, and many more things to do with outer space. He was indeed a very clever man. He also knew he had nothing to fear from the greater intelligences that filled his mind with all manner of wondrous things. They brought with them great feelings of peace and love. He was also aware of the many different life forms that communicated with him.

It was quite rare to find a soul on the earthplane, so eager to learn of all the things that existed in outer space. He continued to receive messages, and in so doing, made many friends with other beings, who fondly called him the earth man who seeks!

It was a relationship of knowledge that travelled beyond time and space. It was also too incredible to try to explain to anyone else. Only twice he had tried to tell his friends, but very quickly realised that they couldn't understand what he was on about, and he'd felt he was making a fool of himself, so he decided to keep things to himself. No one would believe him anyway.

There were many times when he was in a state of awe and wonderment at all he was told by his space brothers, as he came to think of them. And when his life was over, and he returned to the heavenly Realms, he remembered all that he'd been told. His memory was crystal clear.

He also knew that he now lived in a world of thought. He could travel anywhere his soul desired, and he wanted to explore other planets. In fact, he wanted to learn as much as he could about his space brothers that had helped him so much during his life on the earthplane.

He set off with his spirit guide to accompany him, to a planet far out in the solar system. They travelled many light years beyond time and space, as it's known on the earthplane, but in reality, it was a very different energy field altogether from physical energy on the earthplane. There are many very different vibrations of energy that exist in the Universe, and each has its own way of communication.

They arrived at a place that his guide had suggested that should appeal to him. They were welcomed by the space brothers he had communicated with during his life on the earthplane. It was a most uplifting experience. His guide had also been on other visits and was quite well known.

It was a time of learning, and it gave great joy to the scientist to have so many of his questions answered by his many space friends. They were very wise and kind, and very spiritual friends indeed. And he was very proud to know them.

He knew that he had been well respected amongst his colleagues during his working life as a scientist, but his knowledge was like a drop in the ocean compared to their vast and seemingly endless knowledge.

In time they moved on and explored many other places throughout the galaxies, much to the joy and delight of the scientist. All he wanted to do was learn as much as he could. There was no end to his enthusiasm in the search for knowledge.

When he had absorbed as much knowledge as he could, he decided to have a rest and ponder on all he had experienced.

After a brief sojourn, he came to a decision, and he knew exactly what he wanted to do. He wanted another life experience on the earthplane. He longed to share all he had learnt with others and be of service in any way possible to all mankind.

He chose the time and the place and his parents, who agreed during their sleep state to accept him into their lives as their son.

As the years passed, and he grew up into a fine young man, he couldn't remember on a conscious level any of his previous experiences. But his subconscious mind, which is at soul level, had all the information stored there.

When a person is born on the earthplane, all prior knowledge is wiped off the memory banks, to be returned when the physical life is over and the soul returns to another state of consciousness in the spirit world. If this was not so, there would be great confusion, if a soul living a physical life remembered everything from start to finish! Having said this, there are many very advanced souls who do remember a very great deal of their past lives.

It's all part of a very intricate pattern, woven into the divine plan of each soul's journey into perfection, which eventually returns to the infinite wisdom of the creator.

There are some people who feel a restless urge to travel to distant lands and faraway places, and when they visit a certain place, it feels so familiar to them. Yet, they have never to their knowledge, been there before.

This is called Karmic memory, when snippets of past life memories invade this life, leaving a feeling of déjà vu. There can be a feeling of fondness for the place, or intense dislike, depending on the past life experiences in the particular place, that is still filled with memories of the past. They have no effect on the present situation, and should be accepted for what they are, a past life memory.

Let me give you an example. Margaret Clark feels so uncomfortable in a certain place, that she can't bear to visit or even think about it. She realises that she had a very unpleasant experience there in a previous life, and has no desire to go anywhere near the place, knowing full well the reason why.

But let us assume that Margaret has also lived many lives in Egypt, and she feels an irresistible urge to go there. When she eventually visits Egypt, and the sounds, sights and smells engulf her, it all feels so wonderfully familiar. A feeling of happiness and sense of belonging overwhelms her, and she knows that she had a very happy past life there with her family and friends.

The answer to all problems lies within the soul. It's the guiding force in everyone's life. It is also the lever to get one out of tricky situations, when someone has been hasty or foolish over something, and not listened to the voice of their soul.

There are a lot of misconceptions on the earthplane about the soul and God. The soul is part of God. The guiding force that runs through all creation. There are many religious fanatics who believe that God is one person who will forgive them their sins. God does not judge, neither does he dictate, and by asking for forgiveness at a church meeting, and singing a few hymns is not the answer.

This is the wrong way to go about it. But it is all part of the learning process, and no judgement is ever made. Patience, tolerance and love is the answer, and eventually they will realize the truth for themselves. Look within and there is the answer.

CHAPTER TEN

Alien Visitors

There is another world that exists quite close to the earthplane that I haven't mentioned, and the creatures that live there are very happy, harmless little souls indeed. They are beings of light and of great intellect. They make frequent visits to the earthplane to learn more about the people who also exist there. They're rather like neighbours visiting next door.

These lovely beings are of a higher vibration than the earthplane. Their world is also very beautiful. They can't be seen by the physical eye, or touched by the physical hand of a person on the earthplane. Nevertheless, they do exist.

They communicate by telepathy on all levels. It has often amused them in the past when they have seen someone speak through their mouth! It has created much merriment amongst them. Although they understand perfectly that in time the mouth won't be needed to communicate.

These creatures that visit the earthplane from time to time, mean no harm to anyone. They just wish to explore and seek for further knowledge, and will help anyone in need.

I shall describe them to you. They are approximately three feet high, of a greyish hue, with large shaped heads, no mouth and large dark eyes, almost black. They are adept space travellers and very popular visitors to other planets in the solar system, and welcomed wherever they go, because they are so filled with light and radiate a very powerful feeling of love.

These lovely creatures are so benevolent to all they meet, and have been of great help to many other life forms that exist throughout the Universe.

They can see into many other worlds, with different vibrations. The extent of their knowledge would be of great help to those on the earthplane.

These lovely beings never get upset or angry about anything, because they have gone beyond arguments. All is peace and love between them. They exude such loving feelings for others in the Universe, regardless of shape, colour or size, or from which planet they come from, because they know all life is sacred.

They are seldom seen on the earthplane, but there are some psychics who are aware of these little extraterrestrials, and communication has taken place, much to the astonishment of a soul living on the earthplane. When this happens it's an incredible experience to see the interchange of energies and the different flow of colours that pass between them.

This is because colours reflect the personality of the speaker. They also reflect the degree of knowledge they have, and their true feelings are also seen quite clearly, so any attempt to tell lies is pointless, because the truth is always seen for what it truly is!

The beautiful colour vibrations that exist everywhere in the Universe are wonderful to behold, and many a soul has been overjoyed and at times quite overwhelmed just to see them.

Yet, light and darkness walk hand in hand, dark thoughts also have their own vibration, which is usually not a very pleasant sight to see at all.

Thoughts of great wisdom are bathed in soft hues of purple and violet, enveloped in rays of pure white. Thoughts of matter, for example, flowers, have their own vibrating colours, all beautiful, even weeds vibrate beautifully, and their energy field is quite something to behold.

The grass is frequently different shades of green on planet earth, and also vibrates as do the trees, each has its own colour vibration.

There are a multitude of very striking colours in the Universe that many can see at will, and others can't see at all because they are all vibrating at different levels of understanding.

It's untapped knowledge for many on the earthplane, but in time, all will learn of the many benefits and healing values there are in the mixture of colours that vibrate in the Universe. Although there are some wise souls on the earthplane who are aware that colour plays an important part when used in the healing field.

The healing rays of the sunshine is also very therapeutic, even with a hole in the ozone, which isn't as large as some people suggest.

There are certain laws in the Universe, and one of them is that all life is sacred. The second one is that love conquers everything. And the third one is that all knowledge is shared, and no one is above anyone else. All have the right to the truth on all levels.

Jesus said, 'Do unto others as you would be done by.'

I am The Eternal Spirit, who has passed on vital information for all on the earthplane, who wish to learn of things that exist in the Universe.

Everything I have written is the absolute truth. And I would now like to thank Margaret Clark for holding the pen and allowing these writings to flow from the spirit world, which is where I exist.

It is a plane of such wondrous beauty and almost perfection, and one day Margaret shall join me in the Realms of Heaven.

This book is to be called Alpha and Omega by the Eternal Spirit. And Margaret, I would like you to add your name beneath what I have just written. Go in peace my very dear friend until we meet again in Paradise. Margaret Clark.

End

POSTSCRIPT

In my next book, I shall explore the possibilities of what happens when the harmful rays of the sun penetrate the ozone.

It is sometime since I first became aware that I was able to communicate with many other life forms in the Universe, and certain facts shall be explained.

For instance, how these space creatures operate certain things in their worlds, and how they work and live amongst themselves, and how their extraterrestrial thought forms penetrate most galaxies.

I now wish all my readers good health, peaceful thoughts and a very tranquil passing into the Kingdom of Heaven. And may God's Blessing be with you always.

The Eternal Spirit.